# AMERICA

## AN AERIAL CLOSE UP

**Text by Rupert O. Matthews**
CLB 1262
© 1986 Illustrations and text: Colour Library Books Ltd.,
   Guildford, Surrey, England.
Text filmsetting by Acesetters Ltd., Richmond, Surrey, England.
All rights reserved.
1986 edition published by Crescent Books, distributed by Crown Publishers, Inc.
Printed in Spain.
ISBN 0 517 46013 0
h g f e d c b a

# AMERICA
## AN AERIAL CLOSE UP

Text by
**Rupert O. Matthews**

**CRESCENT BOOKS**
**NEW YORK**

The great, sparkling ocean spreads out to the horizon, as it has done for millions of years. The sunlight catches the wave peaks, reflecting back in the same way that it dazzled the earliest settlers four centuries ago. But a thin ribbon of white spray stretched across the deep, blue ocean betrays the presence of man. At the head of the ribbon, always pushing it forward as it disintegrates behind, is one of the many pleasure craft which cross the waters off the east coast of America.

On a warm summer morning the density of the craft surging out of the various harbors and inlets along the coast is astounding. They stream from the marinas around New York City like the spreading struts of some enormous fan, and return in the evening like a thousand white streamers sucked down a funnel. The multitude of tiny craft which form such a feature of the summer scene on the Atlantic coast are an indication of the vast numbers of people who live on the land beyond. It is along this thin strip of land that perhaps the greatest concentration of humanity on the continent is found. Mighty cities crowd in upon one another, their suburbs almost touching. New York, Baltimore, Philadelphia, and a host of others, provide home and work for the millions who live here. At their centers the cities soar like man-made mountain crags to heights which could make them a serious threat to any unwary bird. The giant buildings rise sheer from the water's edge and dwarf the automobiles and buses which weave along the roads between them.

Further out from the city hubs the buildings become the low-lying structures of the commuter belt. Here the streets are broader and the buildings far from obvious, hidden as they are beneath the branches of the trees which line and interweave the streets and roads. The

suburbs could almost give the impression of endless tracts of untouched forest were it not for the freeways, which carve swathes through the land, and their junctions which reveal centers of population.

The great interstates which run between major cities also twist inland across a landscape increasingly broken and rugged. The ground rises, first in low fluctuations then in great ridges of rock, to form the mighty Appalachians. Running from the Atlantic and the Canadian border southwestward into the continent, the long, parallel valleys and peaks form one of the most distinctive landscapes in the east. The snow-capped peaks of the highest mountains stand out like pristine napkins on the green and brown patchwork of the land. Much used by skiing enthusiasts in the winter months, the mountains have been shaped to cater to the sport. Huge pathways down the slopes have been cleared of trees to provide an uninterrupted course where great speeds can be attained. During the summer months, when the crowds have gone with the snows, the fabulous ski runs are nothing more than scars on the dark forests which blanket the mountain slopes.

And beneath the dark forest canopy flowing water catches the sunlight, reflecting it like myriad ever-shifting mirrors. Leaping in sparkling cascades down the steep slopes, the babbling streams carry the water from the melting snows and falling rain away from the heights and down on their long journey to the sea. Following age-old courses, far more ancient than even the mighty mountains, the streams run off in different directions. Long before the massive forces thrust the rocks upwards to form the mountains, rivers ran across the landscape of eastern America. As the beds of rock, thousands of feet thick, began to rise, twist and buckle, the rivers continued to flow. The torrent of water was everywhere so great, that the rivers cut canyons and gullies along which to flow on their old courses as the mountains rose. North of Virginia the rivers still run eastward to the Atlantic, just as they always have. But to the south they run westward to join one of the world's great water systems: the Mississippi.

The streams and brooks which fall down the slopes of the Appalachians join to form broad, powerful rivers which snake away to the west. Growing in strength and power with every mile, the broad flows move ever southwestwards, collecting water from the land they pass and the countless streams which join them on their way. Winding between the farms, villages and towns of the valleys, the rivers were long the main lines of transport. When the first farmers crossed the Appalachians to escape the crowding of their fellows to the east, they moved their goods on flat-bottomed craft along the rivers, and an artificial river, the Erie Canal, had to be built to link them with the east.

With time, the lands to the south and west emerged from the wilderness and became more than blank spaces on the maps of the nation. The great rivers were traversed and mapped, and were found to be as good downstream as up. The broad ribbons of blue which are today empty of all but the occasional pleasure craft, would then have been thick with smoke-belching monsters churning the river behind them. When the waters from the mountains join the flow which began far to the north at Lake Itasca, they create the most majestic river in the nation, the broad Mississippi. Even today this river snakes its tortuous path to the ocean as it always did. Appearing as a great python enfolding fields and houses within its loops, it is still filled with

commercial vessels on its lower courses. The great city of New Orleans, on the shores of the mighty river, throngs with barges and tugs which are a feature of the river for miles downstream and upstream of the town.

Beyond the great north-south run of the Mississippi, fresh rivers reach out across land far different from that to the east. In place of the ridges and hills, revealing fresh views as each is passed, there is only the long, empty stretch of the plains. An unvarying panorama of flatness reaches westwards from the banks of the Father of Waters. The rivers flow here, though, providing landmarks on an otherwise monotonous sea of waving grain and endless roads. Reflecting the square-mile based system of land distribution in the last century, the roads meet at right angles and often take the long way round to a destination, so long as the rigid geometric pattern is not broken. Occupying the great squares and rectangles, which are marked out by the roads and the endless miles of barbed wire, are the spreading fields which make the Great Plains. During the long winter months the land lies barren beneath a blanket of snow, and even the strict pattern of roads can disappear beneath the frozen water. Even when the cold cloak of winter thaws, the land is brown and bare, until the fresh, green shoots poke between the clods. At first appearing as a green haze on the face of the plains, the grain grows until it covers the land almost as completely as the snow. When the green turns to gold and the gentle winds of late summer stir the stalks, the plains almost disappear. The ground seems to twist and writhe as the air stirs the corn and it becomes an endlessly shifting haze on which it is almost impossible to focus.

But the Plains are not a single huge blanket of shifting

grain. Scattered like islands are the marks of man: gas stations at intervals on the highways, and farm buildings, with the inevitable grain elevators, served by the ribbons of steel carrying the trains which make it all possible. As the Plains reach further and further to the south and west, features other than the roads and elevators mark the way. Huge rock formations rise sheer from the land. Many hundreds of feet high, Ship Rock stands alone on the broad expanse of the Plains. So tall and isolated are these features that guides leading wagons trains could navigate by them for days, much as sailors use the stars. For days the rock would lie ahead of the wagons until they reached it, only to mark the horizon behind for days more.

Eventually, the monotony of the Plains breaks in the southwest in the face of geological forces so great they can hardly be imagined. Over a period of millions of years a great dome of rock covering parts of three states was gradually lifted more than a mile into the sky, until the ancient, pre-Cambrian core of the continent lay far above sea level. Here, as in the Appalachians far to the northeast, the old rivers in existence before the uplift were strong enough to continue on their old courses by cutting through the uplifting rock. But here there is a difference. There is little rainfall and the climate is so severe as to allow little plant life. The low rainfall means that there is little erosion at work, other than the rivers. The lack of vegetation creates a desert landscape in which windblown sand and grit can play a part in erosion far different from that played by water. While the rivers have cut down, the upper levels have been left largely intact, and the sides of the valleys have not been rounded off by falling rain. The result is a vast network of canyons which criss-crosses the entire southwest. A seemingly-level plain will suddenly drop away into an abyss so deep that it staggers the imagination. More than a mile deep in sheer rock walls, a powerful torrent of silt-laden water will sparkle in the hot desert sun as it gouges out yet more rock.

The greatest of them all, of course, is the Grand Canyon of northern Arizona. The surging waters of the Colorado River have cut down through more than a mile of rock, exposing the geologic history of the world over more than a hundred million years. Elsewhere along its course the Colorado has been dammed by man to create vast resevoirs. Impressive as are the feats of man, they are nothing to the works of nature.

In other parts of the Southwest the arid conditions have created some of the most beautiful natural rock formations anywhere. In places salt deposits underlie the surface rock, and when this is eroded by the constant drip of underground water, the surface features collapse. In the Needles District of Utah this has created long, parallel ridges of stone cut by deep, straight valleys. Into the soft rocks of the ridges the minimal rain which falls and the constant shifting of temperatures, together with wind-borne grit, have carved delicate figures of tortuous formations, and in places rock has been undermined and pierced to form natural bridges and arches as spectacular from the air as from the ground.

Even the force which uplifted the dome of rock through which the canyons run is feeble compared to earth convulsions which rocked the western states over a period of millions of years. When dinosaurs walked the earth, western North America was fairly low and level. Then the earth moved. Powerful earthquakes and volcanic eruptions, which still shake the region today, began to reshape the land. Fault lines opened up in the earth and massive sections of the rock were moved. The geological history of the western states is complicated and violent, so much so that few scientists even pretend really to understand what happened here. The results, however, are all too obvious.

Rising sheer from the broad, flat expanse of the plains, a wall of rock climbs thousands of feet into the sky. Perhaps it is at its most dramatic in Wyoming, where the Teton Mountains leap from the prairie like the walls of fairytale castles, complete with turrets and towers. Beyond the first dramatic wall of rock lie even taller, more rugged peaks beckoning the traveler. Romantic valleys lie hidden in the heart of vast mountain ranges which unfold across the continent. At Yosemite, impossibly tall and sheer mountains dominate a valley floor which lies spread at their feet like a blanket of vegetation, and a thin trail of falling water marks the stream which cascades into the valley and on.

The mighty Rockies are one of the most outstanding features of the land. They spread across more of the country, climb higher into the sky and plunge deeper into the earth than any other natural feature. In their highest reaches the mountains push so high into the thin atmosphere that the snow on their peaks never melts, and glaciers of frozen ice flow, inch by inch, down their flanks. In the mountain valleys, spread like green trails between the bare, rocky heights, flourish forests and meadows with a wildlife unique to the region: forests so impenetrable that they are rumored to be home to a creature often seen, but never captured – the

Bigfoot. Indeed it is often these man-apes which are said to do the capturing, and more than one lone prospector has told how he had to run for his life.

The same geological rendings which threw up the mountains had quite the opposite effect in a localized southern region of the Rockies. Here the pressures ripped away the support for a massive block of rock which then simply sank into the depths of the earth. Surrounded by peaks many thousands of feet tall, Death Valley lies decidedly below sea-level. Robbed of any rainfall by the peaks which surround it, the valley lies like a vast, flat, brown plain. Almost devoid of life it lies motionless at the foot of its depression.

The mountains march on westward in endless ranks of majestic peaks until they reach the sea. Here there is no broad plain, as in the east. The mountains just drop into the ocean and the land is at an end. The people who live here have to cluster around the few valleys which reach the ocean and cling to the hillsides not too steep to build upon. Built around its broad, natural bay, San Francisco enjoys perhaps the best site of them all. Yet even here the streets climb gradients unheard of elsewhere and the mountain wilderness is never far inland. Beyond, the deep, swelling ocean runs unhindered and unbroken across hundreds of miles of empty scenery until the latest state in the Union comes into sight: Hawaii. Nestled in the bosom of the waters the islands have the air of a paradise into which man has wandered. From coast to coast and beyond, America is a beautiful country, and a country which lies waiting to enchant each and every visitor.

Alaska. Previous page: the sheer-walled peak of Mount McKinley, at 20,320 feet the highest mountain in the North American Continent. The mountain stands some 120 miles from Anchorage (facing page), the largest city in Alaska and the financial and business center of the state. Above: a section of the Trans-Alaska Pipeline south of Fairbanks. Overleaf: (left) the Harding Icefield and (right) the Ruth Glacier on the slopes of Mount McKinley.

Alaska. These pages: snow and ice surrounding the deep, blue waters of Aialik Bay, near Seward. Overleaf: glaciers and snowfields on the slopes of Mount McKinley.

Hawaii. Previous pages: (left) the Koolau Mountains and (right) the soaring cliffs of the Pali Coast which in places
rise to 3,000 feet above the crashing surf around their bases. Facing page: Waikiki and the Ala Wai Yacht Harbor. Above:
Honolulu and Mamala Bay. Overleaf: (left) the island of Molokini and (right) the sheer cliffs of the Hamakua Coast.

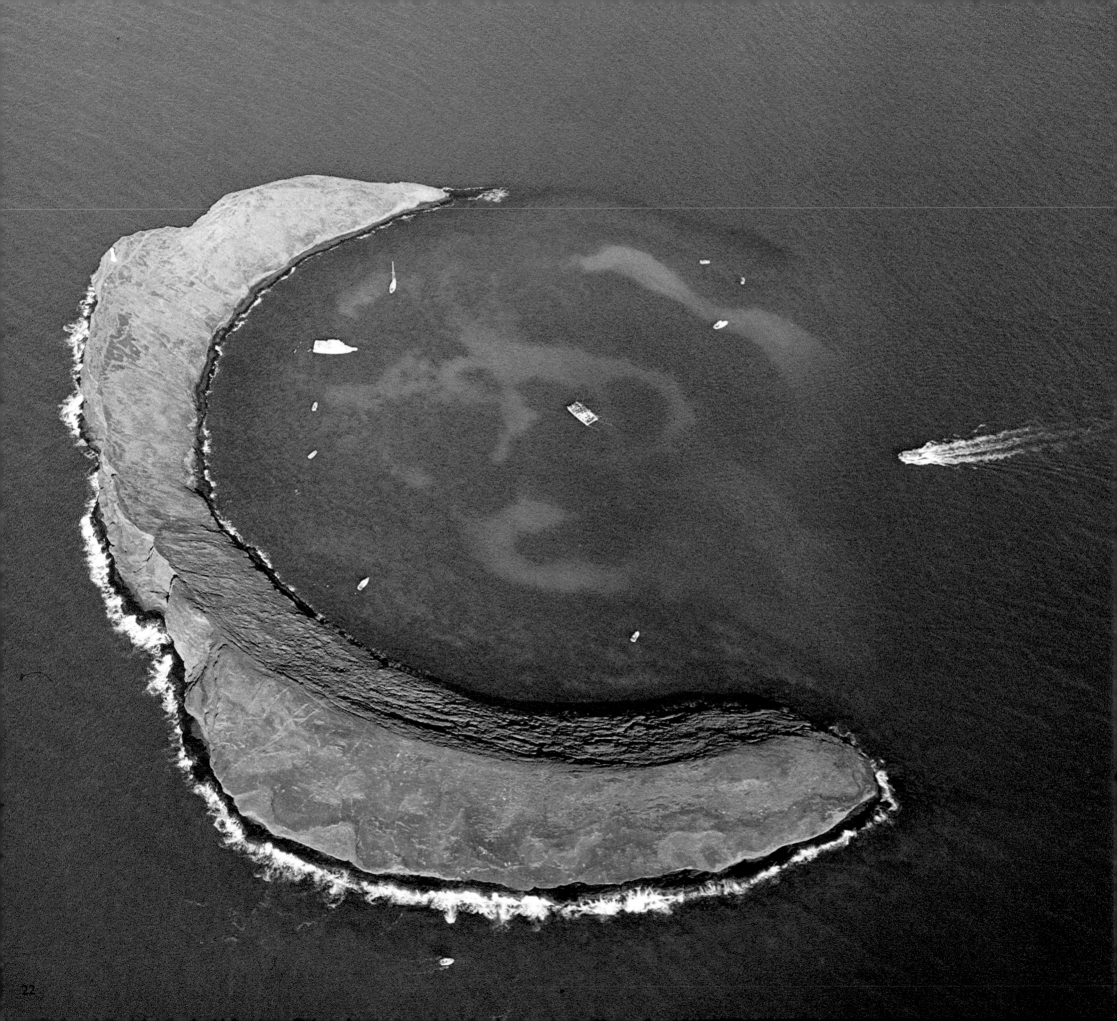

Hawaii. The Koolau Mountains (previous pages left) and (previous pages right) a dramatic waterfall in Hona Kane Valley.
Maine. Cape Elizabeth Lighthouse (above), near Portland; (facing page) the colorful pier at Orchard Beach; (overleaf
left) the State House, designed by Charles Bulfinch, in Augusta, and (overleaf right) the small village of North
Monmouth.

Maine. These pages: Boothbay Harbor, which is crowded with visitors in the summer, but strangely quiet during the winter. Overleaf: (left) the blue waters of Lake Cobbosseecontee, near Monmouth, and (right) Yarmouth, near Portland.

# DUDLEY PUBLIC LIBRARIES

The loan of this book may be renewed if not required by other readers, by contacting the library from which it was borrowed.

27/5/22

Maine. Above: the small port of Friendship, famous for its trim little craft. Facing page: a bridge at South Bristol Harbor. Overleaf: (left) quiet homes and clear waters between Rockland and Spirit Island and (right) the fishing village of Port Clyde.

New Hampshire. Above: forest-surrounded North Conway, in Carroll County. Facing page: Conway, which lies in the east of the state. Overleaf: (left) the magnificent Mount Washington Hotel at Bretton Woods, one of the White Mountains' best-equipped hotels, and (right) Crawford Notch, in the heart of the White Mountains.

New Hampshire. Above: the terminal of the mountain railroad which scales Mount Washington, where in 1934 winds of 234 miles per hour were recorded. Facing page: North Conway, where an old-style railroad adds to the skiing attractions.

New Hampshire. Above: a small lake enfolded in a quiet, wooded valley in the White Mountains. Facing page: a lakeshore house on Lake Winnipesaukee. Overleaf: (left) the White Mountains near Highway 16 and (right) the State House and central Concord.

44

Vermont. Above: an isolated home near Morrisville, in the north of the state. Facing page: a rural town east of Lake Champlain. Overleaf: (left) the granite State Capitol with its gilded dome and (right) the junction of State Street and Main Street, both in Montpelier.

Vermont. Facing page: the town of Morrisville, in the Green Mountains. Above: woodland and fields in the Walden Heights area. Overleaf: (left) the center of Burlington, which is now the largest city in the state, and (right) Hyde Park.

Vermont. Facing page: West Hardwick. Above: a farm near West Danville. Overleaf: (left) part of the magnificent
variation of color which comes to Vermont in the fall and (right) St. Johnsbury, which lies on the Moose and Passumpsic
Rivers.

Vermont. These pages: picturesque rural scenes near St. Johnsbury. Overleaf: (left) Killington, one of the state's largest ski resorts, with six connected mountains, and (right) the town of Rutland, which gained prosperity during the last century.

Boston, Massachusetts. Above: the Weeks Memorial Bridge crosses the Charles River to Harvard University. Facing page:
the First Church of Christ, Scientist, home of the Christian Science Church. Overleaf: (left) the Charles River, with
the tall downtown buildings breaking the horizon, and (right) the Back Bay area of Boston.

Massachusetts. Facing page: the white steeple of Old North Church, where Paul Revere had his two lanterns displayed on
April 18, 1775, dominates this view of Boston. Above: the buildings of Harvard University in Cambridge.

Massachusetts. Above: Provincetown seen from the northwest, with Race Point in the foreground. Facing page: beach-side houses in Provincetown. Overleaf: (left) Cape Poge and (right) Lighthouse Beach with Eel Pond beyond, at Edgartown, both on Martha's Vineyard.

Massachusetts. Above: the 352-foot-tall Pilgrim Monument in Provincetown, which commemorates the Pilgrim Fathers' short stop here in 1620 before moving on to Plymouth. Facing page: the coastline near Brewster. Overleaf: (left) boats moored at the eastern end of Martha's Vineyard and (right) Provincetown and the curving hook of Long Point.

Rhode Island. These pages: the magnificent Newport Bridge, which crosses Narragansett Bay from Newport to Jamestown.
Overleaf: (left) the highly-indented shoreline around Brenton Point and (right) some of the magnificent turn-of-the-
century mansions for which Newport is justly famous.

Rhode Island. Facing page: the State Capitol in Providence, which is often considered the loveliest in the nation and boasts the second-largest marble dome in the world. Above: a panoramic view of Providence. Overleaf: (left) Newport Harbor and (right) Thames Street and the main downtown area of Newport.

83

Connecticut. Hartford (these pages and overleaf) is the largest city in the state as well as the capital, and it is also one of the most charming, with its broad streets and extensive parks. At the heart of the city stands the magnificent State Capitol (facing page), built of local marble, with its golden dome and many statues. Overleaf left: City Hall.

Connecticut. Until a few years ago the skyline of Hartford was low and gentle, with few structures breaking the pattern.
Today, however, the city center is easily distinguishable from the rest of the city by its tall buildings (above).
Facing page: the cathedral.

Connecticut. Above: the silky blue waters of Ocean Beach, near New London. Facing page: the Harkness Memorial State Park, near Goshen Point, with its 42-room mansion and 200 acres of grounds. Overleaf: Mystic, showing (left) the swing bridge on Main Street and (right) Mystic Seaport, a recreated sea-faring village of the last century.

New York. Above: the chateau-style State Capitol and the more modern Rockefeller Empire State Plaza in Albany. Facing page: the Mohonk Mountain House at New Paltz, one of the finest hotels in the state. Overleaf: the city of Buffalo, an important inland port on Lake Erie.

New York. Previous pages: the tiny *Maid of the Mist* boat noses into the turbulent waters beneath Niagara's Horseshoe
Falls. Above and overleaf: the soaring skyline of Manhattan. Facing page: the guiding beacon of the light atop the
Statue of Liberty marks the entrance to New York Harbor.

New York. Above: Central Park, some 800 acres of landscaped greenery, which serves as a haven for city dwellers. Facing page: the sparkling lights of Manhattan brighten a nighttime scene.

Long Island, New York. Above: the beautiful sweep of sand at Long Beach. Facing page: a narrow neck of land, crowded with seaside homes and with Long Island Sound beyond, at Asharoken.

Long Island, New York. Above: Fire Island Lighthouse and the Robert Moses State Park with Kismet and Saltaire in the distance. Facing page: Southampton Beach and tennis club. Overleaf: (left) Jones Beach and (right) the Lido Hotel.

New Jersey. As the second-largest city in the state, Jersey City (these pages and overleaf left) gains much of its importance from its proximity to New York City. Overleaf right: Atlantic City, which has regained much of its 19th-century glamor and prosperity since casinos were sanctioned in 1976.

New Jersey. Facing page: the beautiful autumnal colors which cover the land around Trenton airfield in the fall. Above:
a line of arches carries a viaduct over the Delaware River. Overleaf: Trenton, on the Delaware River, is the capital of
New Jersey and houses the gold-domed State House of 1792.

Pennsylvania. Philadelphia is one of the most historic cities in the nation, for it was here that the Declaration of
Independence and the Constitution were signed. Above and facing page: Benjamin Franklin Parkway leads past Logan Circle
to the graceful columns of the Museum of Art. Overleaf: (left) scaffolding encloses the tower of City Hall and (right)
the *Gazela of Philadelphia* lies moored at Penns Landing.

Pennsylvania. These pages: views of the battlefield at Gettysburg, perhaps the most decisive battle in the Civil War, where fighting raged for three days before General Lee and his Confederate troops were forced to retreat. Overleaf: the forested slopes of Pennsylvania's Grand Canyon.

Pennsylvania. These pages: the Golden Triangle of Pittsburgh, where the Ohio River is born out of the confluence of the Allegheny and Monongahela. An area of much recent rebuilding and reconstruction, the Golden Triangle is the heart of this powerful city.

Delaware. Above: farmland near Wilmington. Like many colonial cities, Dover was laid out around a green and this still survives together with the white-roofed State House (facing page). Overleaf: (left) Highway 13 passing through Smyrna and (right) farmland near Dover.

Maryland. Previous pages left: Annapolis, capital of Maryland and a city which can trace its roots back to the middle of the 17th. century. Previous pages right, these pages and overleaf: Baltimore, the largest city in the state, was founded in 1729 and has long been an important port and industrial center. Overleaf: (left) the Washington Monument and (right) the Gothic National Bank building.

Maryland. Above, facing page and overleaf left: the magnificent buildings of the United States Naval Academy at Annapolis, which has been the Navy's undergraduate college for nearly 150 years. Overleaf right: the dramatic engineering feat of the Bay Bridge over Chesapeake Bay.

Maryland. Facing page: the City Dock and Main Street of Annapolis, with the gray and white spire of the State House in the background. Above: the Bethlehem Steelworks at Sparrow Point, Baltimore.

District of Columbia. At the heart of the national capital stands the home of the President. The White House (these pages) was begun in 1792, but was never finished as originally planned due to constant interruptions, one of which was its burning by the British in 1814, after which it was whitewashed and thus gained its name.

West Virginia. Above: one of many small rivers which tumble through the beautiful autumnal shades that blanket the hills during the fall. Facing page: a town in northern West Virginia.

Virginia. Previous pages: (left) farmland near Greenfield and (right) Monticello, the beautiful home of Thomas Jefferson, which he began in 1769. These pages: Virginian landscapes around Chesapeake Bay. Overleaf: Williamsburg, the recreated capital of colonial Virginia, with (left) the Governor's Mansion and (right) the Magazine and Guardhouse.

Kentucky. These pages and overleaf left: the George Rogers Clark and J.F. Kennedy Memorial Bridges cross the Ohio River, linking Louisville, the largest city in Kentucky, with Indiana. Overleaf right: the State Capitol of 1909 in Frankfort, built in Indiana limestone, contains statues of Abraham Lincoln and Jefferson Davis, both native Kentuckians.

Kentucky. Famous for its horse breeding and raising, Kentucky has many monuments to fine horseflesh. Facing page: the Churchill Downs, Louisville, where the famous Kentucky Derby is run each May, after a spectacular ten-day festival. Above: a racetrack outside Lexington.

Kentucky. The bluegrass of the state has long been considered as the best in the nation on which to graze horses, and the expertise of horsebreeders in Kentucky is hard to match. Throughout the state studfarms and stables proliferate, as around Lexington (these pages and overleaf).

Tennessee. These pages: downtown Chattanooga. Overleaf: (left) the campus of the Memphis State University and (right) a view from above Mud Island across the Wolf River toward downtown Memphis.

North Carolina. Previous pages: the magnificent, forest-covered landscape of the Great Smoky Mountains, perhaps the most beautiful area of the state. Above: St. Mary's College, Raleigh. Facing page: the Classical State Capitol in Raleigh.
Overleaf: (left) the State Legislative Building in Raleigh and (right) a farm near Raleigh airport.

Columbia, South Carolina. Above: the football stadium of the University of South Carolina. Facing page: the "Horseshoe" area of South Carolina University. Overleaf: (left) a silver dome caps the red-brick hospital buildings on the outskirts of the city and (right) the granite State House which was begun in 1851, damaged by cannon during the Civil War and finally completed in 1907.

South Carolina. These pages and overleaf left: the neatly laid-out paddocks and buildings of Coughman Farms, an extensive horse farm 15 miles east of Columbia. Overleaf right: some of the historic buildings in the Battery section of Charleston.

Charleston, South Carolina. Above: tennis courts beside Colonial Lake. Facing page and overleaf left: the Battery district. Overleaf right: the fine episcopal church of St. Michael's, which dates back to 1751, when it was considered one of the finest churches in the North American colonies.

Charleston, South Carolina. Above: houses lining the shores of Colonial Lake. Facing page: the historic Battery area, where some of the loveliest old homes of the city are located.

Atlanta, Georgia. Previous pages: (left) a football stadium and (right) the modern, high-rise buildings of the downtown area. These pages: the wealth and prosperity of the new Atlanta is symbolised in the height and magnificence of the office blocks which dominate the center of the city. Overleaf: (left) Stone Mountain, centerpiece of a park where the city's young gather in the summer months, and (right) the gilded dome of the Capitol.

Florida. Miami Beach (these pages and overleaf), the vacation wonderland of southeastern America, with its 10-mile-long sandy beach, golf courses and fine hotels.

Above: Alabama's State Capitol in Montgomery, a city of beautiful ante-bellum architecture and thrusting, modern buildings. Facing page: Fort Lauderdale, Florida.

Mississippi. These pages: the city of Jackson, capital of the state, was almost totally destroyed during the Civil War, in July, 1863, and took many years to recover. It was only during this century that Jackson really regained its lost prosperity as new railroads and a natural gasfield aided the growth of industry.

Missouri. Previous pages: (left) the Gateway Arch, which dominates the city of St. Louis from a height of some 630 feet, and (right) the Busch Memorial Stadium. These pages: Although a great manufacturing city, Kansas City (these pages), contains thousands of acres of parks and has some fine, carefully-planned residential districts. Overleaf: (left) the Capitol in Jefferson City and (right) the University of Missouri in Columbia.

Louisiana. New Orleans is one of the most intriguing cities in America. Its modern wealth and prosperity can be seen in the tall buildings and busy roads which abound throughout the city (previous pages, above and overleaf right), while its elegant French traditions and strong jazz atmosphere can still be savored in the Vieux Carré (facing page and overleaf left).

Arkansas. Above: the dome of the granite and marble State Capitol rises above the city of Little Rock. Facing page: the Arkansas River winds between hills, while Little Rock lies in the distance.

Illinois. Chicago (these pages and overleaf), on the shores of Lake Michigan, is the second largest city in the nation. Its citizens, however, point to their past achievements and present vitality and prosperity and claim that their city ought, perhaps, to take first place.

Illinois. These pages: the open spaces of Naveland Park and Zoo, where the inhabitants of Chicago can relax and forget the worries of the big city. Overleaf: (left) Lake Shore Drive and (right) the North Golden Coast, both in Chicago.

Indiana. One of the most famous scenes in Indianapolis (these pages) is the Indianapolis Motor Speedway (above) which is the venue for what it proudly declares to be the largest sporting event in the world, the Indianapolis 500.

Ohio. These pages: the Great Lakes port of Toledo is situated on Lake Erie, where the Maumee River spills its waters into the lake. As well as a port of prime importance, the city is also a large commercial and industrial center.

Michigan. Detroit (these pages and overleaf) is a city which has long been identified with automobile manufacture, and is still, to a large extent, dependent upon that industry. Above: a cargo ship moves up the Detroit River. Facing page the Renaissance Center. Overleaf: (left) the downtown area and (right) an island in the Detroit River.

Madison, Wisconsin. The neck of land which separates Lake Mendota from Lake Monona has been carefully laid out to form a
rigid street plan at the center of which stands the Capitol (these pages and overleaf right), often considered to be one
of the most imposing in the nation. Overleaf left: the university football stadium.

239

Wisconsin. Facing page: the Wisconsin River at the Dells, where the flow of water has carved fantastic shapes from the rocks. Above: the view from Point Lookout in the Wyalusing State Park.

242

owa. With 200,000 inhabitants, Des Moines (previous pages and these pages) is the largest city in the state. At its
heart stands the gold-domed Capitol (previous pages left), whose original foundation stone, laid in 1870, had to be
replaced after three years because it was faulty. Overleaf: nearby farming land.

Minnesota. The Twin Cities (these pages and overleaf) are the industrial and financial heart of the state. Above: Lake Harriet, with the towers of downtown Minneapolis beyond. Overleaf right: downtown Minneapolis. Facing page and overleaf left: the older and more conservative city of St. Paul.

Minnesota. Facing page: the spreading suburbs of Minneapolis. Above: the green-roofed City Hall is overshadowed by more recent high-rise buildings in Minneapolis. Overleaf left: the University of Minnesota on the banks of the Mississippi. Overleaf right: the white dome of the Capitol and the green dome of the Cathedral are just visible in this view of St. Paul.

North Dakota. Bismarck (above and overleaf) has grown steadily since it became the state capital in 1889, and houses a distinctive State Capitol (overleaf left), which was built in 1932. Facing page: the restored blockhouses of nearby Fort Abraham Lincoln, from which General Custer marched out to his death in 1876.

South Dakota. Where the Big Sioux River tumbles over rocks stands the aptly-named Sioux Falls (these pages and overleaf), the largest city in the state. Though it was abandoned in 1862 after threats of an Indian attack, the city has developed steadily and is now an important center for the surrounding agricultural land.

South Dakota. Above: an almost unearthly landscape in the Badlands National Park, one of the most recent additions to the national parks system, having been established in 1978. Facing page: the far more productive farmland to be found in Walworth County.

Nebraska. Lincoln (these pages) became state capital in 1867, at a time when only 30 people lived there; today it has a population approaching 200,000. Above: the University of Nebraska. Facing page: the State Capitol of 1922. Overleaf: rich farmland and broad rivers typical of the landscapes between Omaha and Lincoln.

Nebraska. Omaha (these pages) is barely a century old, the land having been opened up to White settlement following a treaty with the Omaha Indians in 1854. Above: the colorful Rosenblatt Stadium. Facing page: Central Park Mall between Douglas and Farnham Streets.

Kansas. Previous pages and overleaf: the fertile farmland around Wichita in the southern part of the state. These pages:
Wichita, the largest and most important city in the state, makes its contribution to the arts with the blue-domed
Century II Cultural Center (facing page).

Oklahoma. Previous pages and above: downtown Oklahoma City, which was settled almost overnight when the territory was opened up last century. Facing page: the State Capitol, in front of which stands Constance Warren's famous *Statue of a Cowboy*, and its adjacent complex. Overleaf: farmland north of the city.

283

Texas. For nearly a century Dallas (these pages and overleaf) prospered as an agricultural and pastoral center before the discovery of oil in the 1930s transformed it into the bustling, exciting city that it is today. Facing page and overleaf right: the soaring Reunion Tower stands beside the gleaming, black Hyatt Regency Hotel.

ROADWAY

287

Texas. Facing page: Southfork Ranch. Above: modern jets cluster about the terminal at the Dallas Fort Worth Airport.
Overleaf: (left) the White Water amusement park between Dallas and Fort Worth and (right) the Wet and Wild Water Park, situated just off Interstate 30 near Dallas.

Texas. These pages and overleaf: Fort Worth started life as an isolated military post in 1849 and has changed its role many times since; it has been a cattle town, agricultural center and, more recently, an oil town. But throughout all the changes the city has maintained its frontier spirit, a feeling evident even today.

295

Texas. Above: the magnificent, 570-foot-tall masonry monument at San Jacinto where, on April 21, 1836, 800 Texans under General Sam Houston defeated 1,500 Mexicans and captured the dictator Santa Anna, thereby gaining freedom for Texas. Facing page: downtown Houston, the largest city in the state.

Texas. Corpus Christi (these pages and overleaf right) has a diversified economy in which natural gas and seafood play prominent roles. The city is built around Corpus Christi Bay, which was discoverd by a Spanish explorer on the feast day of Corpus Christi in 1519. Overleaf left: neatly plowed farmland near Corpus Christi.

300

Above: the shattered ruins of Fort Union, New Mexico, which protected the Santa Fe trail for 40 years until it was abandoned in 1891. Facing page: Tucson, Arizona, which is one of the oldest towns in the Southwest, dating back to a Spanish settlement of 1776. Overleaf: the industrial and agricultural center of Phoenix, state capital of Arizona.

Arizona. Lying in a valley where temperatures top 100 degrees most summer days, Phoenix (these pages) has grown quickly since the introduction of air conditioning and is now an important industrial and agricultural city. Overleaf: Biltmore, where irrigation has turned the desert into a green and fruitful place.

Arizona. Previous pages: (left) the mighty Hoover Dam, which is 726 feet tall and holds back the waters of Lake Mead, at 115 miles long one of the largest artificial lakes in existence, and (right) the Black Canyon below the dam. These pages and overleaf: the Grand Canyon.

The Grand Canyon (these pages), Arizona, is one of the most spectacular geologic sights in the world. The Colorado River has been cutting away at the rock for thousands of years to create the yawning chasm which is some 5,700 feet deep and 250 miles long. Overleaf: (left) the Colorado River between Dead Horse Point and The Loop, and (right) the Confluence of the Colorado and Green Rivers, both in Utah.

Utah. Previous pages: the desert town of Moab, which lies tucked away in its valley beside the Colorado River. Above: scaffolding encases the tower of Salt Lake City's City and County Building. Facing page: mineral works at Potash, on the Colorado River. Overleaf: the marble and granite State Capitol Building in Salt Lake City.

Colorado. Above and overleaf right: scenically-sited Colorado Springs houses three major military bases: the U.S. Air Force Academy, Fort Carson, and Peterson Air Force Base. Facing page: Denver, with its gold-domed Capitol. Overleaf left: the campus of the University of Colorado at Boulder.

Colorado. These pages: the spectacular and dramatic Red Rocks, which rise from a valley floor a few miles south of
Denver. Overleaf: winter in Colorado brings heavy snows which blanket the high mountains, such as these near Aspen.

Colorado. Facing page: the mountain town of Aspen, which was once a silver mining center but now makes its living as a ski resort. Above and overleaf right: Vail, one of the most popular skiing venues in the state, was originally built in the style of an Alpine resort. Overleaf left: Marble Ski Resort.

Colorado. Overleaf left: roads cleared of snow trace intricate brown tracks through the white landscape at Snowmass Ski Resort. These pages and overleaf right: nearby snow-capped peaks.

341

Wyoming. Above: the fine Corinthian Capitol, built in 1887, which stands at the head of Capitol Avenue in Cheyenne (overleaf). Facing page: the University of Wyoming in Laramie, the state's third largest city.

Wyoming. The various aspects of the state's economy can be gaged from its landscapes: (above) strip farming west of
Cheyenne; (facing page) an oil shale pit near Cheyenne; (overleaf left) a river snakes tortuously through grass meadows
in the Red Mountain area and (overleaf right) a nearby stand of timber.

348

These pages: melting winter snows decorate Wyoming's Snowy Mountains, where the narrow roads are much used by visitors to view the impressive beauty of the range. Overleaf: (left) McDonald Creek and the towering face of Garden Wall in Glacier National Park and (right) a cowboy at work, both in Montana.

Idaho. These pages: the patchwork farming land which characterizes the extreme southwest of the state, where the lowlands surrounding the Boise and Snake Rivers join. Overleaf: Boise, capital and financial heart of Idaho, takes its name from the French word for woodland, *bois*, a name given to this forested site by early French trappers.

357

Idaho. Although most of Idaho is covered by mountain, forest or desert, it as an agricultural area that the state is best known. Large irrigation projects have turned dry lands into productive fields, (these pages and overleaf left) southwest of Boise. Overleaf right: artificially cleared pathways between the trees on a hill north of Boise reveal the presence of a winter ski resort.

Nevada. Largely desert or sparse grazing land, Nevada has to rely mainly on tourism for its prosperity. The greatest boost to tourism was given in 1931, when gambling was legalized. Since that time Las Vegas (these pages and overleaf) has boomed, as casinos and hotels proliferated to cater for the gambling visitors.

Nevada. Trapped behind the towering wall of the Hoover Dam is Lake Mead (these pages), which provides much-needed irrigation water to the surrounding countryside. A less essential, but more enjoyable, use for the lake has been found by the boating fraternity, as the craft at Lake Mead Marina (facing page) testify.

California. San Diego (previous pages, these pages and overleaf) stands on the site of a Spanish mission founded in 1769, the earliest in California. Previous pages: (left) the financial district and (right) the luxurious Hotel del Coronado and the sweep of the San Diego-Coronado Bay Bridge. Facing page: pleasure craft in the harbor. Above: the financial district. Overleaf: (left) a golf course on the Coronado Peninsula, and (right) La Jolla.

California. Facing page: a stream finds its way to the Pacific across the golden sands of Pacific Palisades, north of
Los Angeles. Above: the huge liner *Queen Mary*, which is now moored at Pier J, Long Beach, and houses many interesting
exhibits. Overleaf: (left) Los Angeles' Memorial Coliseum, venue for the 1932 and 1984 Olympics, and (right) Universal
Studios, which offers tours around the movie sets.

California. Above: the luxurious Beverly Hills Hotel. Facing page: Los Angeles from the southwest. Overleaf: (left) the Hollywood Bowl and (right) the J. Paul Getty Museum in Malibu, built in the style of an ancient Roman villa.

378

California. Above: the Nevada Falls and, below them, the Vernal Falls in Yosemite National Park. Facing page: the lava beds of Painted Dunes. Overleaf: (left) the soft, but forbidding, sand dunes which cover much of Death Valley and (right) the view from Zabriskie Point.

California. Facing page: Highway 1 arcs across a graceful bridge some 260 feet above Bixby Creek. Above: a view from Chimney Rock in the Point Reyes National Seashore. Overleaf: (left) cattle and a tractor in a field of stubble near Livermore and (right) the golf course on Cypress Point.

California. Previous pages, these pages and overleaf: the city of San Francisco is one of the most beautifully-situated cities in America, and at the same time one of the best known. The city's vitality and exuberance are felt by all who visit it, as is the beauty of its surroundings.

California. Above: a ship glides along a canal, between fertile fields, near Sacramento. Facing page: Sacramento, with the dome of the Capitol, completed in 1874, standing amid a patch of greenery.

California. Above: the clear, green waters of Lake Tahoe at D.L. Bliss State Park. Facing page: the steaming landscape of Bumpass Hell in Lassen Volcanic National Park, which covers 163 square miles of northern California.

Oregon. Facing page: Portland, the largest city in the state, stands near the confluence of the Columbia and Willamette Rivers. Above: the conical Wizard Island in Crater Lake. The view from the summit of Mount Bachelor (overleaf left) includes the summits of Three Sisters and Broken Top (overleaf right).

Washington. Seattle (these pages and overleaf) lies on the shores of Puget Sound and has a metropolitan population well in excess of a million, making it the main city of the Pacific Northwest. Perhaps the most famous feature of this fine port is the tower known as the Space Needle (overleaf right) which dominates the skyline.

Washington. Previous pages: (left) farm buildings near the Green River and (right) prestigious waterside homes at Bellevue, near Seattle. Above: the canyon carved by the Palouse River on its way to meet the Snake. Facing page: undulating Palouse farming country. Overleaf: Glacier Peak breaks the skyline in the Cascades.

# INDEX

Aialik Bay, Alaska    14, 15
Albany, New York    96
Anchorage, Alaska    11
Annapolis, Maryland    136, 142, 143, 144, 146
Asharoken, New York    109
Aspen, Colorado    334
Atlanta, Georgia    192 – 195, 197
Atlantic City    117
Augusta, Maine    28

Badlands National Park, South Dakota    264
Baltimore, Maryland    137 – 141, 147
Bellevue, Washington    409
Beverly Hills, California    378
Biltmore, Arizona    308, 309
Bismarck, North Dakota    257 – 259
Bixby Creek, California    386
Black Canyon, Arizona    311
Boise, Idaho    356, 357
Boothbay Harbor, Maine    30, 31
Boston, Massachusetts    64 – 68
Boulder, Colorado    328
Brenton Point, Rhode Island    80
Bretton Woods, New Hampshire    40
Broken Top, Oregon    403
Buffalo, New York    98, 99
Burlington, Vermont    54

Cambridge, Massachusetts    69
Cape Elizabeth Lighthouse, Maine    26
Cape Poge, Massachusetts    72
Charleston, South Carolina    185 – 191
Chattanooga, Tennessee    168, 169
Chesapeake Bay Bridge, Maryland    142
Cheyenne, Wyoming    342, 344, 345
Chicago, Illinois    220 – 227
Churchill Downs, Kentucky    162
Colorado River, Utah    318
Colorado Springs, Colorado    326, 329
Columbia, Missouri    211
Columbia, South Carolina    178 – 181
Concord, New Hampshire    47
Confluence, The, Utah    319
Conway, New Hampshire    39
Corpus Christi, Texas    298, 299, 301
Coughman Farms, South Carolina    182 – 184
Crater Lake, Oregon    401
Crawford Notch, New Hampshire    41
Cypress Point, California    389

D.L. Bliss State Park, California    398
Dallas Fort Worth Airport, Texas    289

Dallas, Texas    284 – 287
Death Valley, California    384, 385
Dells, the, Wisconsin    240
Denver, Colorado    327
Des Moines, Iowa    242 – 245
Detroit, Michigan    232 – 235
Dover, Delaware    133

Edgartown, Massachusetts    73

Fire Island Lighthouse, New York    110
Fort Abraham Lincoln, North Dakota    256
Fort Lauderdale, Florida    203
Fort Union, New Mexico    302
Fort Worth    292 – 295
Frankfort, Kentucky    161
Friendship, Maine,    34

Gettysburg, Pennsylvania    126, 127
Glacier National Park, Montana    352
Glacier Peak, Washington    412
Grand Canyon, Arizona    312 – 317
Grand Canyon, Pennsylvania    128, 129
Great Smoky Mountains, North Carolina    172, 173

Hamakua Coast, Hawaii    23
Harding Icefield, Alaska    12
Harkness Memorial State Park, Connecticut    93
Hartford, Connecticut    86 – 91
Hollywood Bowl, California    380
Hona Kane Valley, Hawaii    25
Honolulu, Hawaii    21
Hoover Dam, Arizona    310
Houston, Texas    297
Hyde Park, Vermont    55

Indianapolis, Indiana    228, 229

Jackson, Mississippi    204, 205
Jefferson City, Missouri    210
Jersey City, New Jersey    114 – 116
Jones Beach, New York    112

Kansas City, Missouri    208, 209
Killington, Vermont    62
Koolau Mountains, Hawaii    18, 24

Lake Cobbosseecontee, Maine    32
Lake Mead, Nevada    366, 367
Lake Tahoe, California    398
Lake Winnipesaukee, New Hampshire    45
Laramie, Wyoming    343

Las Vegas, Nevada    362 – 365
Lassen Volcanic National Park, California    399
Lincoln, Nebraska    266, 267
Little Rock, Arkansas    218, 219
Long Beach, California    375
Long Beach, New York    108
Los Angeles, California    376, 377, 379
Louisville, Kentucky    158 – 160

Madison, Wisconsin    236 – 239
Malibu (J. Paul Getty Museum), California    381
Marble Ski Resort, Colorado    336
Memphis, Tennessee    170, 171
Miami Beach, Florida    198 – 201
Minneapolis, Minnesota    248, 251, 252, 253
Moab, Utah    320, 321
Mohonk Mountain House, New York    97
Molokini, Hawaii    22
Montgomery, Alabama    202
Monticello, Virginia    153
Montpelier, Vermont    50, 51
Morrisville, Vermont    52
Mount Bachelor, Oregon    402
Mount MacKinley, Alaska    9, 13, 16, 17
Mount Washington, New Hampshire    42
Mystic, Connecticut    94
Mystic Seaport, Connecticut    95

New Orleans, Louisiana    212 – 217
New York, New York    102 – 107
Newport Bridge, Rhode Island    78, 79
Newport, Rhode Island    81, 84, 85
Niagara Falls, New York    100, 101
North Conway, New Hampshire    38, 43
North Monmouth    29

Ocean Beach, Connecticut    92
Oklahoma City, Oklahoma    278 – 281
Omaha, Nebraska    270, 271
Orchard Beach, Maine    27

Pacific Palisades, California    374
Painted Dunes, California    383
Pali Coast, Hawaii    19
Palouse River, Washington    410
Philadelphia, Pennsylvania    122 – 125
Phoenix, Arizona    304 – 307
Pittsburgh, Pennsylvania    130, 131
Point Reyes National Seashore, California    387

Port Clyde, Maine    37
Portland, Oregon    400
Potash, Utah    323
Providence, Rhode Island    82, 83
Provincetown, Massachusetts    70, 71, 74, 77

Race Point, Massachusetts    70
Raleigh, North Carolina    174 – 176
Red Rocks, Colorado    330, 331
Rutland, Vermont    63

Sacramento, California    397
Salt Lake City, Utah    322, 324, 325
San Diego, California    368 – 373
San Francisco, California    390 – 395
San Jacinto, Texas    296
Seattle, Washington    404 – 407
Sioux Falls, South Dakota    260 – 263
Smyrna, Delaware    134
Snowmass Ski Resort, Colorado    340
Snowy Mountains, Wyoming    350, 351
South Bristol Harbor, Maine    35
Southfork Ranch, Texas    288
Southampton, New York    111
St. Johnsbury, Vermont    59
St. Louis, Missouri    206, 207
St. Paul, Minnesota    249, 250, 255
Stone Mountain, Georgia    196

Three Sisters, Oregon    403
Toledo, Ohio    230, 231
Trenton, New Jersey    120, 121
Tucson, Arizona    303

Vail, Colorado    335, 337

Waikiki, Hawaii    20
Walden Heights, Vermont    53
Walworth County, South Dakota    265
Washington, D.C.    148, 149
West Hardwick, Vermont    56
West Virginia    150, 151
White Mountains, New Hampshire    44, 46
Wichita, Kansas    274, 275
Williamsburg, Virginia    156, 157
Wyalusing State Park, Wisconsin    241

Yarmouth, Maine    33
Yosemite National Park, California    382